JOHN BEECHER, although a great-great-nephew of Abolitionists Henry Ward Beecher and Harriet Beecher Stowe, was brought up in Birmingham, Alabama, where his father was an executive of U.S. Steel. From the age of 14 when he finished high school, John Beecher worked in steel mills. Twelve-hour shifts on the open hearth furnaces turned him into a rebel and a poet.

He attended VMI, Cornell and the University of Alabama, was a graduate student at Harvard and the University of North Carolina, and traveled in Europe for a year. After teaching at Dartmouth and the University of Wisconsin, where he was on the staff of Dr. Alexander Meiklejohn's famous Experimental College, Beecher for eight years administered New Deal programs in the South, dealing with the rural and urban poor, migratory labor, and Negroes discriminated against in employment. Among his posts was that of regional director for President Roosevelt's original Fair Employment Practice Committee.

During World War II Beecher served aboard the racially integrated Liberty ship, "Booker T. Washington," and wrote a book, *All Brave Sailors*, which Earl Conrad called in the *Chicago Defender,* "a milestone in literature and politics . . . the strongest stuff to come out of the war."

Beecher was an editor in Washington, D.C. following the war and later taught at San Francisco State College. Refusing to sign the unconstitutional Levering Act oath adopted by the State of California in 1950, he became a working rancher. He and his wife founded a private press to print his poetry, winning several awards.

In 1958 Beecher moved to Arizona, teaching at Arizona State University. From 1963 to 1965 he was Poet in Residence at the University of Santa Clara in California. He is presently Visiting Professor at Miles College, a Negro institution in Birmingham. Besides his activities as a poet, Beecher is an associate editor of *Ramparts,* a contributor to national magazines, and is writing a study of the contemporary South which Macmillan will publish.

D1244049

John Beecher

TO
LIVE AND DIE
IN DIXIE

& OTHER POEMS

Red Mountain Editions
mcmlxvi

ACKNOWLEDGMENTS:

The narrative poem, *IN EGYPT LAND*, was originally published in a limited Rampart Press edition. Most of the other poems appeared first in *Brand X, Caravel, Commonweal, Continuum, Fellowship, Folio, Hawk and Whippoorwill, Literary Art Press, Mainstream, Minority of One, Morning Star Quartos, National Guardian, Omnibus, The Owl, renaissance, Rights, Social Digest,* and *Way.* Thanks where due for permission to reprint. Translations of several into Spanish, Russian and Greek have been published in *Siempre!* (Mexico City), *Literaturnaya Gazeta* (Moscow), *Nea Estia* (Athens) and *Tachydromos Egyptos* (Alexandria). "A Veteran's Day of Recollection" was included in the recent anthology, *POETS OF TODAY*, edited by Walter Lowenfels. A number of the poems were also assembled in *UNDESIRABLES*, a pamphlet of my work published by the Goosetree Press in its New Poets series. Special gratitude is expressed to James Singer, the editor and publisher. Four of the poems herein are taken from my *LAND OF THE FREE*, a 1956 collection now out of print. J. B.

Book design and block prints by Barbara Beecher.

RED MOUNTAIN EDITIONS
Box 7331-A   Mountain Brook Station
Birmingham, Alabama 35223

In Memoriam

Leonard Thurlow Beecher

1867 - 1959

> *Men must endure*
> *Their going hence, even as their coming hither;*
> *Ripeness is all.*

CONTENTS

ALSO BY JOHN BEECHER:

I

IN
EGYPT
LAND

I

It was Alabama, 1932
but the spring came
same as it always had.
A man just couldn't help believing
this would be a good year for him
when he saw redbud and dogwood everywhere in bloom
and the peachtree blossoming
all by itself
up against the gray boards of the cabin.
A man had to believe
so Cliff James hitched up his pair of old mules
and went out and plowed up the old land
the other man's land but he plowed it
and when it was plowed it looked new again
the cotton and corn stalks turned under
the red clay shining with wet
under the sun.

Years ago
he thought he bought this land
borrowed the money to pay for it
from the furnish merchant in Notasulga
big white man named Mr Parker
but betwixt the interest and the bad times coming
Mr Parker had got the land back
and nigh on to $500 more owing to him
for interest seed fertilize and rations
with a mortgage on all the stock -
the two cows and their calves
the heifer and the pair of old mules -
Mr Parker could come drive them off the place any day

if he took a notion
and the law would back him.

Mighty few sharecroppers
black folks or white
ever got themselves stock like Cliff had
they didn't have any cows
they plowed with the landlord's mule and tools
they didn't have a thing.
Took a heap of doing without
to get your own stock and your own tools
but he'd done it
and still that hadn't made him satisfied.
The land he plowed
he wanted to be his.
Now all come of wanting his own land
he was back to where he started.
Any day
Mr Parker could run him off
drive away the mules the cows the heifer and the calves
to sell in town
take the wagon the plow tools the store-bought furniture
    and the shotgun
on the debt.
No
that was one thing Mr Parker never would get a hold of
not that shotgun ...

Remembering that night last year
remembering the meeting
in the church he and his neighbors always went to
deep in the woods
and when the folks weren't singing or praying or
    clapping and stomping

you could hear the branch splashing over rocks
right out behind.
That meeting night
the preacher prayed a prayer
for all the sharecroppers
white and black
asking the good Lord Jesus
to look down
and see how they were suffering.
"Five cent cotton Lord
and no way Lord for a man to come out.
Fifty cents a day Lord for working in the field
just four bits Lord for a good strong hand
from dawn to dark Lord from can till can't
ain't no way Lord a man can come out.
They's got to be a way Lord show us the way . . . "
And then they sang.
"Go Down Moses" was the song they sang
"Go down Moses, way down in Egypt land
Tell old Pharaoh to let my people go"
and when they had sung the song
the preacher got up and he said
"Brothers and sisters
we got with us tonight
a colored lady teaches school in Birmingham
going to tell us about the Union
what's got room for colored folks and white
what's got room for all the folks
that ain't got no land
that ain't got no stock
that ain't got no something to eat half the year
that ain't got no shoes
that raises all the cotton
but can't get none to wear

'cept old patchedy overhauls and floursack dresses.
Brothers and sisters
listen to this colored lady from Birmingham
who the Lord done sent I do believe
to show us the way . . ."

Then the colored lady from Birmingham
got up and she told them.
She told them how she was raised on a farm herself
a sharecrop farm near Demopolis
and walked six miles to a one-room school
and six miles back every day
till her people moved to Birmingham
where there was a high school for colored
and she went to it.
Then she worked in white folks' houses
and saved what she made
to go to college.
She went to Tuskegee
and when she finished
got a job teaching school in Birmingham
but she never could forget
the people she was raised with
the sharecrop farmers
and how they had to live.
No
all the time she was teaching school
she thought about them
what could she do for them
and what could they do for themselves.
Then one day
somebody told her about the Union . . .

14

If everybody joined the Union she said
a good strong hand would get what he was worth
a dollar (Amen sister)
instead of fifty cents a day.
At settling time the cropper could take his cotton to
        the gin
and get his own fair half and the cotton seed
instead of the landlord hauling it off and cheating on
        the weight.
"All you made was four bales Jim" when it really was six
(Ain't it God's truth?)
and the Union would get everybody the right to have
        a garden spot
not just cotton crowded up to the house
and the Union would see the children got a schoolbus
like the white children rode in every day
and didn't have to walk twelve miles.
That was the thing   .
the children getting to school
(Amen)
the children learning something besides chop cotton
        and pick it
(Yes)
the children learning how to read and write
(Amen)
the children knowing how to figure
so the landlord wouldn't be the only one
could keep accounts
(Preach the Word sister).

Then the door banging open against the wall
and the Laws in their lace boots
the High Sheriff himself
with his deputies behind him.

Folks scrambling to get away
out the windows and door
and the Laws' fists going *clunk clunk clunk*
on all the men's and women's faces they could reach
and when everybody was out and running
the pistols going off behind them.
Next meeting night
the men that had them brought shotguns to church
and the High Sheriff got a charge of birdshot in his body
when Ralph Gray with just his single barrel
stopped a car full of Laws
on the road to the church
and shot it out with their 44's.
Ralph Gray died
but the people in the church
all got away alive.

16

II

The crop was laid by.
From now till picking time
only the hot sun worked
ripening the bolls
and men rested after the plowing and plowing
women rested
little boys rested
and little girls rested
after the chopping and chopping with their hoes.
Now the cotton was big.
Now the cotton could take care of itself from the weeds
while the August sun worked
ripening the bolls.

Cliff James couldn't remember ever making a better crop
on that old red land
he'd seen so much of
wash down the gullies toward the Tallapoosa
since he'd first put a plow to it.
Never a better crop
but it had taken the fertilize
and it had taken work
fighting the weeds
fighting the weevils . . .
Ten bales it looked like it would make
ten good bales when it was picked
a thousand dollars worth of cotton once
enough to pay out on seed and fertilize and furnish
    for the season
and the interest and something down
on the land

new shoes for the family to go to church in
work shirts and overalls for the man and boys
a bolt of calico for the woman and girls
and a little cash money for Christmas.

Now though
ten bales of cotton
didn't bring what three used to.
Two hundred and fifty dollars was about what his share
    of this year's crop would bring
at five cents a pound
not even enough to pay out on seed and fertilize and
    furnish for the season
let alone the interest on the land Mr Parker was asking
    for
and $80 more on the back debt owing to him.
Mr Parker had cut his groceries off at the commissary
    last month
and there had been empty bellies in Cliff James' house
with just cornbread buttermilk and greens to eat.
If he killed a calf to feed his family
Mr Parker could send him to the chain-gang
for slaughtering mortgaged stock.

Come settling time this fall
Mr Parker was going to get every last thing
every dime of the cotton money
the corn
the mules
the cattle
and the law would back him.
Cliff James wondered
why had he plowed the land in the spring
why had he worked and worked his crop

his wife and children alongside him in the field
and now pretty soon
they would all be going out again
dragging their long sacks
bending double in the hot sun
picking Mr Parker's cotton for him.

Sitting on the stoop of his cabin
with his legs hanging over the rotten board edges
Cliff James looked across his fields of thick green cotton
to the woods beyond
and a thunderhead piled high in the south
piled soft and white like cotton on the stoop
like a big day's pick
waiting for the wagon
to come haul it to the gin.
On the other side of those woods
was John McMullen's place
and over yonder just east of the woods
Ned Cobb's and beyond the rise of ground
Milo Bentley lived that was the only new man
to move into the Reeltown section that season.
Milo just drifted in from Detroit
because his work gave out up there
and a man had to feed his family
so he came back to the farm
thinking things were like they used to be
but he was finding out different.
Yes
everybody was finding out different
Cliff and John and Ned and Milo and Judson Simpson
        across the creek
even white croppers like Mr Sam and his brother Mr Bill
they were finding out.

It wasn't many years ago Mr Sam's children
would chunk at Cliff James' children
on their way home from school
and split little Cliff's head open with a rock once
because his daddy was getting too uppity
buying himself a farm.
Last time they had a Union meeting though at Milo
    Bentley's place
who should show up but Mr Sam and Mr Bill
and asked was it only for colored
or could white folks join
because something just had to be done
about the way things were.
When Cliff told them
it was for all the poor farmers
that wanted to stick together
they paid their nickel to sign up
and their two cents each for first month's dues
and they said they would try to get
more white folks in
because white men and black
were getting beat with the same stick these days.

Things looked worse than they ever had in all his time
    of life
Cliff James thought
but they looked better too
they looked better than they ever had in all his time
    of life
when a sharecropper like Ralph Gray
not drunk but cold sober
would stand off the High Sheriff with birdshot
and get himself plugged with 44's
just so the others at the meeting could get away

and after that the mob hunting for who started the Union
beating men and women up with pistol butts and bull
    whips
throwing them in jail and beating them up more
but still not stopping it
the Union going on
more people signing up
more and more every week
meeting in houses on the quiet
nobody giving it away
and now white folks coming in too.

Cliff James looked over his ripening cotton to the woods
and above the trees the thunderhead piled still higher
    in the south
white like a pile of cotton on the stoop
piling up higher and higher
coming out of the south
bringing storm . . .

21

III

"You"
Cliff James said
"nor the High Sheriff
nor all his deputies
is gonna git them mules."
The head deputy put the writ of attachment back in his
    inside pocket
then his hand went to the butt of his pistol
but he didn't pull it.
"I'm going to get the High Sheriff and help"
he said
"and come back and kill you all in a pile."

Cliff James and Ned Cobb watched the deputy whirl
    the car around
and speed down the rough mud road.
He took the turn skidding
and was gone.
"He'll be back in a hour" Cliff James said
"if'n he don't wreck hisseff."
"Where you fixin' to go?" Ned Cobb asked him.
"I's fixin' to stay right where I is."
"I'll go git the others then."
"No need of eve'ybody gittin' kilt" Cliff James said.
"Better gittin' kilt quick
than perishin' slow like we been a'doin'" and Ned Cobb
    was gone
cutting across the wet red field full of dead cotton plants
and then he was in the woods
bare now except for the few green pines
and though Cliff couldn't see him

he could see him in his mind
calling out John McMullen and telling him about it
then cutting off east to Milo Bentley's
crossing the creek on the foot-log to Judson Simpson's. . .
Cliff couldn't see him
going to Mr Sam or Mr Bill about it
no
this was something you couldn't expect white folks to
    get in on
even white folks in your Union.

There came John McMullen out of the woods
toting that old musket of his.
He said it went back to Civil War days
and it looked it
but John could really knock a squirrel off a limb
or get a running rabbit with it.
"Here I is," John said
and "What you doin' 'bout you folks?"
"What folks?"
"The ones belongin' to you.
You chillens and you wife."
"I disremembered 'em," Cliff James said.
"I done clean disremembered all about my chillens and
    my wife."
"They can stay with mine," John said.
"We ain't gonna want no womenfolks nor chillens
not here we ain't."

Cliff James watched his family going across the field
the five backs going away from him
in the wet red clay among the dead cotton plants
'and soon they would be in the woods
his wife

young Cliff
the two girls
and the small boy . . .
They would just have to get along
best way they could
because a man had to do
what he had to do
and if he kept thinking about the folks belonging to him
he couldn't do it
and then he wouldn't be any good to them
or himself either.
There they went into the woods
the folks belonging to him gone
gone for good
and they not knowing it
but he knowing it
yes God
he knowing it well.

When the head deputy got back
with three more deputies for help
but not the High Sheriff
there were forty men in Cliff James' cabin
all armed.
The head deputy and the others got out of the car
and started up the slope toward the cabin.
Behind the dark windows
the men they didn't know were there
sighted their guns.
Then the deputies stopped.
"You Cliff James!" the head deputy shouted
"come on out
we want to talk with you."
No answer from inside.

24

"Come on out Cliff
we got something we want to talk over."
Maybe they really did have something to talk over
Cliff James thought
maybe all those men inside
wouldn't have to die for him or he for them...
"I's goin' out," he said.
"No you ain't," Ned Cobb said.
"Yes I is," Cliff James said
and leaning his shotgun against the wall
he opened the door just a wide enough crack
for himself to get through
but Ned Cobb crowded in behind him
and came out too
without his gun
and shut the door.
Together they walked toward the Laws.
When they were halfway Cliff James stopped
and Ned stopped with him
and Cliff called out to the Laws
"I's ready to listen white folks".

"This is what we got to say nigger!"
and the head deputy whipped out his pistol.
The first shot got Ned
and the next two got Cliff in the back
as he was dragging Ned to the cabin.
When they were in the shooting started from inside
everybody crowding up to the windows
with their old shotguns and muskets
not minding the pistol bullets from the Laws.
Of a sudden John McMullen
broke out of the door
meaning to make a run for his house

and tell his and Cliff James' folks
to get a long way away
but a bullet got him in the head
and he fell on his face
among the dead cotton plants
and his life's blood soaked into the old red land.

The room was full of powder smoke and men groaning
that had caught pistol bullets
but not Cliff James.
He lay in the corner quiet
feeling the blood run down his back and legs
but when somebody shouted
"The Laws is runnin' away!"
he got to his feet and went to the door and opened it.
Sure enough three of the Laws
were helping the fourth one into the car
but it wasn't the head deputy.
There by the door-post was John McMullen's old musket
where he'd left it when he ran out and got killed.
Cliff picked it up and saw it was still loaded.
He raised it and steadied it against the door-post
aiming it at where the head deputy would be sitting
to drive the car.
Cliff only wished
he could shoot that thing like John McMullen . . .

IV

He didn't know there was such a place in all Alabama
just for colored.
They put him in a room to himself
with a white bed and white sheets
and the black nurse put a white gown on his black body
after she washed off the dried black blood.
Then the black doctor came
and looked at the pistol bullet holes in his back
and put white bandages on
and stuck a long needle in his arm
and went away.

How long ago was it
he stayed and shot it out with the Laws?
Seemed like a long time
but come to think of it
he hid out in Mr Sam's corn crib
till the sun went down that evening
then walked and walked all the night-time
and when it started to get light he saw a cabin
with smoke coming out the chimney
but the woman wouldn't let him in to get warm
so he went on in the woods and lay down
under an old gum tree and covered himself with leaves
and when he woke up it was nearly night-time again
and there were six buzzards perched in the old gum tree
watching him . . .
Then he got up and shooed the buzzards away
and walked all the second night-time
and just as it was getting light
he was here

and this was Tuskegee
where the Laws couldn't find him
but John McMullen was dead in the cotton field
and the buzzards would be at him by now
if nobody hadn't buried him
and who would there be to bury him
with everybody shot or run away or hiding?

In a couple of days it was going to be Christmas
yes Christmas
and nobody belonging to Cliff James
was going to get a thing
not so much as an orange or a candy stick
for the littlest boy.
What kind of a Christmas was that
when a man didn't even have a few nickels
to get his children some oranges and candy sticks
what kind of a Christmas and what kind of a country
        anyway
when you made ten bales of cotton
five thousand pounds of cotton
with your own hands
and your wife's hands
and all your children's hands
and then the Laws came to take your mules away
and drive your cows to sell in town
and your calves
and your heifer
and you couldn't even get commissary credit
for coffee molasses and sow-belly
and nobody in your house had shoes to wear
or any kind of fitting Sunday clothes
and no Christmas for nobody. . .

"Go Down Moses" was the song they sang
and when they had finished singing
it was so quiet in the church
you could hear the branch splashing over rocks
right out behind.
Then the preacher got up and he preached . . .

"And there was a man what fought to save us all
he wropped an old quilt around him
because it was wintertime and he had two pistol bullets
    in his back
and he went out of his house
and he started walking across the country to Tuskegee.
He got mighty cold
and his bare feet pained him
and his back like to killed him
and he thought
here is a cabin with smoke coming out the chimley
and they will let me in to the fire
because they are just poor folks like me
and when I have got warm
I will be on my way to Tuskegee
but the woman was afeared
and barred the door again him
and he went and piled leaves over him in the woods
waiting for the night-time
and six buzzards settled in an old gum tree
watching did he still breathe . . ."

The Sheriff removed Cliff James from the hospital to the county jail on December 22. A mob gathered to lynch the prisoner on Christmas day. For protection he was taken to jail in Montgomery. Here Cliff James died on the stone floor of his cell, December 27, 1932.

II

TO LIVE AND DIE IN DIXIE

TO LIVE AND DIE IN DIXIE

I
Our gang
laid for the kids from niggertown
We'd whoop from ambush chunking flints
and see pale soles
of black feet scampering
patched overalls and floursack pinafores
pigtails with little bows
flying on the breeze
More fun than birds
to chunk at
Birds
were too hard to hit

II
Old Maggie's sweat would drip and sizzle
on that cast iron range she stoked
but she was grinding at the handle
of our great big ice cream freezer
that day she had her stroke
It put a damper on my mother's luncheon
All the ladies in their picture hats and organdies
hushed up until the ambulance took Maggie off
but soon I heard
their shrieks of laughter
like the bird-house at the zoo
while they spooned in
their fresh peach cream

33

III
Asparagus fresh from the garden
my dad insisted
went best on breakfast toast with melted butter
so Rob was on the job by six
He used to wake me whistling blues
and whistled them all day till plumb
black dark when he got off
Times Mother was away
he'd play piano for me
real barrelhouse
(I liked it better than our pianola classics)
and clog on the hardwood floor
Rob quit us once to paper houses on his own
but white men came at night and sloshed
paint all over his fresh-papered walls
took the spark plugs out of his Model T truck
poured sand into the cylinders
then screwed the plugs back in
so when Rob cranked it up next day
he wrecked the motor
He came back to work for us
but I can't seem to remember
him whistling much again

IV
Black convicts in their stripes and shackles
were grading our schoolyard
At big recess we watched them eat
their greasy peas off tin
a tobacco-chewing white man over them
shotgun at the ready
and pistol slung
In class we'd hear them singing at their work

"Go Down Old Hannah"
"Jumpin Judy"
"Lead Me to the Rock"
I found a convict's filed off chain once in the woods
and took it home
and hid it

V
Tired of waiting for Hallowe'en
Jack and I had one ahead of time
and went round soaping windows
and chunking clods of mud on people's porches
Mr. Holcomb though came out shooting
his 45
at us scrouged up against a terrace
across the street
He meant to kill us too
because his fourth shot hit betwixt us
not a foot to spare each way
so we didn't wait for him to empty the magazine
but just aired out a mile a minute
Next day
our mothers made us apologize
and Mr. Holcomb said he wouldn't have shot at us
except it was so dark
he took us for nigger boys

VI
Confederate veterans came to town
for their convention
and tottered in parade
while Dixie played and everybody gave the rebel yell
but the Confederate burying ground near school
where the battle had been

nobody seemed to care about
It was a wilderness of weeds and brambles
with headstones broken and turned over
The big boys had a den in there
where they would drag the colored girls
that passed by on the path
and make them do
what they said all colored girls
liked doing
no matter how much
they fought back and screamed

VII
The Fourth of July
was a holiday for everybody but people's cooks
Corinne was fixing us hot biscuit
when I marched into the kitchen
waving the Stars and Stripes
and ordered her to
"Salute this flag! It made you free!"
I just couldn't understand why Corinne
plumb wouldn't

VIII
Old Major Suggs
ran for Public Safety Commissioner once
orating against the black menace
from his flag-draped touring car
and got just 67 votes
from a town that had 132,685 people in 1910
Things were well in hand back then
and folks were hard to panic
One night a chicken thief got into
old Major Suggs' hen-house

and made off with some of his Barred Rocks
The Major was slick
and figured out the path the thief was sure to take
back to niggertown
so he took a short cut through the woods
and hid behind a tree
The thief came staggering
beneath his sack of hens
and caught both barrels in his face
point-blank
"That nigger flopped and flopped"
old Major Suggs gloated long afterwards
"just like a big black rooster that you've axed"

IX
Spurgeon would daub designs on flowerpots
wheelbarrows
garbage cans
just anything he could get his hands on
though all he had was house-paint
and the kind of big flat brush
you slap it on with
My mother said
Spurgeon was what you call
a primitive
One Saturday evening
he was downtown window-shopping the pawnshops
gawking at all the jewelry
the pretty knives and pistols
when a mob came tearing round the corner
after another black man
but they made Spurgeon do

YOU KIDDING OR SOMETHING WHITE FOLKS?

To the Messrs J. F. & Robt Kennedy Meany Udall et al
Sirs I have been stirred to the depths by your recent sono-
rous pronouncements exhorting the populace to cease &
desist from discriminatory practices against Negroes & since
I have no doubt at all of your individual & collective sincer-
ity I should like to call to your notice an egregious instance
of this evil against which you so eloquently inveigh &
which any one of you individually has ample power to correct but collectively could instantly eradicate by a mere
stroke of the pen as they say Well my wife & I were recently
motoring through the "fair" state of Alabama when in our
road rose gigantic the new Widow's Creek power plant of
the TVA which is an agency of the U S Government De-
ciding to inspect this imposing facility my wife & I each
took a most edifying leaflet from the guard (white) at the
entry We proceeded to the visitors' gallery whence we com-
manded a view of the generators a long row of which were
thrumming in unison except for one which was getting a
new armature Electricians (white) swarmed antlike over the
generator being repaired & as we were intently observing
their activities a black employe of the U S of A came up to
us pushing a broom over the spotless tiles of the gallery
I smiled at him & he smiled back in friendly fashion & I
asked him why he wasn't working down there on the generator with the electricians (white) & the broom-pushing
black smilingly replied though with what I thought was a
touch of irony "You kidding or something white folks?"

"CHAINEY"

The field boss claimed his privilege. Her knife
quenched all his lust for black girls. She got life
in the Big Rock and swung a chain-gang pick
a quarter century before she broke.
To save her keep they kicked her out, paroled.
Root, hog, or die! Thereafter she despoiled
our garbage cans of what our pampered pets
repudiated. We capering white brats
dogged her around, mocking that tethered gait.
She shambled rolling-eyed down every street
in Birmingham, mumbling of "Jedgment." All
our minds were shackled by her chain and ball.

THE CONVICT MINES
Circa 1910

"You sho' God bettah dig yo' task lessen
dat sweat-box git you or yo' bones be foun'
down some ole shaft." At dawn the shackled men,
lamps flaring on their caps, rode underground.
Four bits a day each convict brought on lease,
leading astute police to engineer
crap games to raid. Feeding just pone and peas,
mine owners heaped up fortunes year by year.
Murderers proved most reliable trusties
to stimulate output, wielding the thong
on shirkers and the sick alike. The fees
kept taxes down. Few deemed the system wrong,
it worked so well. Crime profited the state
and reinforced the black mortality rate.

DIXIE BARD

The inexorable anapests of Dixie bard
Stella Foxhall DeRoulhac rode to rescue
white womanhood from brutish blacks. She charred
foiled rapists in slow fires as surely due.
Maternal cares oft frustrating her Muse,
Stella conveyed her daughter's custody
to a half-witted maid. The wench was loose
but never asked for Sundays off at three.
People, said Stella, were just pampering maids.
The half-wit in the bushes held Love's court
when school let out and soon the primary grades
practiced precociously the eldest sport.
Young Stella, barely six, showed future promise
of nymphomania, nor did prediction miss.

MAN OF HONOR

His black barouche swept down the avenue
from his Ionic mansion's porte-cochere,
brisk hooves sounding matutinal tattoo.
Honeysuckle upon sequestered air
giving place to the aroma of pit privies,
he rode, scented silk handkerchief to nose,
by his abutting Negro properties
which squatted rump to rump in squalid rows.
Alighting at his bank's grave porticoes,
our subject laid aside *noblesse oblige*
during banking hours, though never would he foreclose
upon a social equal. Who'd then presage,
himself foreclosed in '29, his shame
would dictate that he sign in blood quit-claim?

FREE WORLD NOTES

I
Lowdown white sonofabitch
comin in here and stirrin up our niggers to vote
lemme at him with this here blackjack
the cops done turned their backs

II
I find you guilty Brenda Travis age 16
of an aggravatin breach of the public peace
for sittin down at the counter
of the bus station cafe
and I therefore sentence you
to one year's imprisonment
in the colored females' reformatory

III
We the coroner's jury bein duly sworn
do find that State Rep'sentative Hurst
did whip Herbert Lee a nigra boy age 52
right smart over the head with the butt of his pistol
and did also fire a 45-caliber projectile
into the nigra's intercranial cavity
such bein the proximate cause of said Herbert's demise
and we do further find and pronounce
this act to have been justifiable homicide
the nigra boy havin provoked the Rep'sentative
unwarrantably
by insistin that he be registered on the book
and permitted to vote like a citizen

THE BETTER SORT OF PEOPLE

Our Negroes here are satisfied
They don't complain about a thing
except the weather maybe
whenever it's too cold to fish
for cat along the riverbank
But when they get away from here
up to Chicago or Detroit
and stay a while and then come back with notions
about the right to vote
or going to school with white folks
we sometimes have to get it through their heads
who runs this country
They're better off down here
or else why don't they stay up yonder?
A lot of them keep coming back
but somehow they've been spoiled
and need the fear of God
thrown into them again
Mind you I'm against the kind of thing
the ignorant rednecks do
I think it was unnecessary
to beat that little Negro boy to death
and throw his body in the Tallahatchie
He was uppity
no doubt about it
and whistled at a white woman
He probably learned that in Chicago
so we ought to make allowances
A good horsewhipping should have been enough
to put him back into his place
and been sufficient warning to him that
if ever he got fresh again

he wouldn't live to see Chicago
Those rednecks that abducted him
I doubt if even they
really meant to kill him when they started
working on him
They just got too enthusiastic
Like I say the better sort of people
down here in Mississippi
we love our Negroes
We wouldn't harm them for the world
This violence you hear so much about
is all the fault of low-down rednecks
poor white trash

A DIXIE HERO

Ole Raymon seed this black boy comin long
the walk an didn' lahk his looks so he
retch down an grab a gre't big rock an stove
damn nigguh's head in faw him. Nevah seed
so comical a thang sence Ah been bawn.
Ole Raymon bust a hole big as a half
a dollah spang in his fo'head. Cain't kill
no nigguh thataway. They skulls is bone
clean th'oo. Well, Raymon got th'owed outa school.
Shit, not faw that. He cussed the principal.

ONE MORE RIVER TO CROSS
For John L. Salter, Jr.

"The passage of the Patowmac through the Blue Ridge"
wrote the author of the Declaration of Independence
"is one of the most stupendous scenes in nature"
In the midst of this stupendous scene
on the second day of December 1859
the sovereign state of Virginia
hanged old Osawatomie Brown
(strange confluence of rivers)
for holding certain truths to be self-evident
which had been first enunciated
by the greatest Virginian of them all
A bystander at the hanging
one Thomas J Jackson
was struck by the incongruity of Brown's
"white socks and slippers of predominating red"
beneath sober black garb more appropriate to the occasion
A frivolous touch that "predominating red"
or could it have been a portent
Thomas J soon-to-be-dubbed "Stonewall" Jackson?
"Across the river and into the trees" you babbled
only four years later
while your blood ebbed away
ironically shot by one of your own
But it is still the second of December 1859
and you glowing with the vigor of a man in his prime
are watching while the body of Brown swings slowly
to and fro
in a cold wind off the mountains
for exactly 37 minutes before it is cut down
In less than half so many months
Thomas J Jackson

44

this stupendous scene plus 24,000 contiguous square miles
will no longer be Virginia
Its blue-uniformed sons will be ranged against you
in the Army of the Potomac singing
"John Brown's body lies a-mouldering in the grave
but his soul goes marching on"

Now you my friend
so akin in spirit to the earlier John
I have been seeing your picture in the papers
your head anointed with mustard and ketchup
at the lunch-counter sit-in
hoodlums rubbing salt in the cuts where they slugged you
or the police flailing you with clubs
blood sopping your shirt
but pure downright peace on your face
making a new kind of history
Now the people Harper's Weekly called
"this good-humored good-for-nothing half monkey race"
when John Brown sought to lead them out of bondage
are leading us toward that America
Thomas Jefferson foresaw and Abraham Lincoln
who once again sprawls dying in his theatre box
(Why must we always kill our best?)
The dastard in the bushes spots the crossed hairs
squeezes the trigger and Medgar Evers pitches
forward on his face while the assassin scuttles
into the night his beady rat's eyes seeking where to hide
his incriminating weapon with the telescopic sight
He heaves it into the tangled honeysuckle
and vanishes into the magnolia darkness
"God Sees the Truth But Waits"
The sickness is loosed now into the whole body politic
the infection spreading from South to North and West

"States Rights" "Freedom of Choice" "Liberty of the
    Individual"
Trojan horse phrases with armed enemies within
In the name of rights they would destroy all rights
put freedom to death on the pretext of saving it
Under the cover of Jeffersonian verbiage
these men move to destroy the Constitution
they feign to uphold
but their plots will miscarry
Who knows but that some unpainted shack in the Delta
may house one destined to lead us the next great step of
    the way
From the Osawatomie to the "Patowmac"
the Alabama Tombigbee Big Black Tallahatchie and Pearl
and down to the Mississippi levee in Plaquemines Parish
it's a long road
better than a hundred years in traveling
and now the Potomac again . . .
    Summer, 1963

WOKE UP THIS MORNING WITH MY MIND SET ON FREEDOM

A flood of song
breaches the levee
swamps cabins in the cotton
sweeps Natchez-under-the-hill

The flock escapes old shepherds
who in the dust of the stampede
incredulous and dazed
lumber along out of breath

46

Frock coats and crinolines
built nothing here
but skilled black hands
reared all this beauty

Which one of these
white-colonnaded bastions of the ancient lie
among moss-oaks and magnolias
will be our Freedom House?
   Natchez during the demonstrations, September, 1965.

ALTER CHRISTUS

Yes I remember him
a truly saintly priest
alter Christus
that is to say *another Christ*
such as we priests are all supposed to be
but yet you know a man like that
can do more mischief than a hundred
of the humdrum usual kind
That trouble he got into
could so easily have been avoided
Foolhardy was the word for him
I remember how for years he set his face
against all plans of his parishioners
to provide him with a car and driver

The Twelve Disciples went on foot he said
so trolleys should be good enough for him
Off he'd go to nowhere on the trolley
all alone and in the dead of night
taking the sacraments to some poor soul
regardless of the danger that he ran
The Ku Klux Klan was capable
of luring him to some abode of vice
on a fake call
and compromising him in people's eyes
thus doing all us priests an injury
The Bishop tried to make him see
the folly of his ways but he
just shook his head and smiled angelically
No harm could come to him he said
on such a holy errand
Our Lord Himself was there to guard him
How innocently trusting he could be!
So when this woman came to him and said
she'd like him to instruct her in the faith
he went ahead despite her character
Why she was a fallen woman
a very Magdalen!
He should have been more prudent
but no he treated her as if she'd been
a bona fide convert
and found a husband for her in the Church
Some kind of foreigner
I never went along with those who claimed
the foreigner had Negro blood
though to be sure his skin was rather swarthy
but still the woman's father had good cause
to feel aggrieved
He was a Klansman

48

a sort of jackleg preacher
who hung around the court house
and eked a living out by marrying couples
hot off the license bureau
Perhaps he felt his business was infringed
Right in broad day he took his gun
The priest was sitting on his porch
reading his breviary for Passion Week
and hearing feet come up the steps
he must have raised his eyes
and looked into the pistol's mouth
Some might consider him a martyr
but do you know
he actually did us all a lot of harm
The murderer was acquitted of his crime
by a jury packed with Klansmen
and the woman didn't even stick
She fell away soon afterwards
They always do that kind
The town believed that there had been
something between the two of them
The whisper went around
and where a priest's involved
such whispers find a ready ear
That's why I always say
we can't be too suspicious
of those who come to us
from lives of public vice and sin
with tears of feigned repentance
The safest thing for us to do
is shut our door against such persons
lest scandal enter in

49

ENSLEY, ALABAMA: 1932

The mills are down.
The hundred stacks
are shorn of their drifting fume.
The idle tracks
rust . . .
Smeared red with the dust
of millions of tons of smelted ore
the furnaces loom —
towering, desolate tubes —
smokeless and stark in the sun . . .
Powerhouse cubes
turbines hummed in,
platesteel mains the airblast thrummed in
are quiet, and the sudden roar
of blown-off steam . . .
At night
the needle gleam
where the ladle poured at the pig machine,
the deep smoulder of an iron run
and the spreading light
of molten slag over the sleeping town
are seen
no more
now mills and men are down.

50

A COMMEMORATIVE ODE

For the 60th Anniversary of the Beecher Memorial
United Church of Christ in New Orleans, Louisiana,
October 25, 1964.

Old church with the same name as my own
you and I were born in the same year
It has taken two generations to bring us together
Now here we are in New Orleans
meeting for the first time
I hope I can say the right thing
what the man you are named for
might have said on one of his better days
He was my great-great-uncle
but come to think of it
he was instrumental in my founding too
Rolled in a tube at home I have a certificate
signed by Henry Ward Beecher
after he had united my grandfather and grandmother
in the holy bonds of matrimony
at Plymouth Church in Brooklyn
The year was 1858
and James Buchanan was President
The South was riding high
making the North catch and send back its escaped Negroes
and it looked to most people
as if slavery were going to last forever
but not to Henry Ward Beecher
which I suppose is why you named your church for him
He certainly helped to change all that
together with his brother Edward and his sister
whose name was Harriet
and Mr. Lincoln and General Ulysses S. Grant

and a large number of young men
who wound up under the long rows of crosses
at Gettysburg Chickamauga Cold Harbor and such places

Nineteen hundred and four was a better year
than 1858
and the building of this church was a sign of it
It was no longer a crime to meet and worship by yourselves
with your own preacher
your own beautiful songs
with no grim-lipped regulators to stand guard over you
nobody breaking up your services with a bull-whip
Yes this was some better
Booker T. Washington was in his hey-day
the apostle of segregation
"We can be in all things social as separate as the fingers"
he said and Mr. Henry Grady the Atlanta editor
applauded him to the echo
as did all the other good white folks around
and they said
"This boy Booker has a head on his shoulders
even if it is a nappy one"
Dr. Washington was 48 years old at the time
but you know how southern whites talk
a man is a boy all his life if he's black
Dr. Washington was a pragmatist
and settled for what he could get
When they announced that dinner was served in the dining
    car
he ate his cindery biscuits out of a paper bag
and when George the porter made up berths in the Pullman
he sat up all night in the Jim Crow coach

Because of his eminently practical attitude
Dr. Washington was successful in shaking down
the big white philanthropists
like C. P. Huntington the railroad shark
or was it octopus
and Negro education was on its way

Old church
since 1904
you and I have seen some changes
slow at first
now picking up speed
I have just come from Mississippi
where I saw churches like this one
burned to the ground
or smashed flat with bombs
almost like Germany when I was there in 1945
only these Negroes were not beaten people
They sang in the ashes and wreckage
such songs as *We Shall Overcome*
and *Let My Little Light Shine*
O Freedom! they sang
Before I'll be a slave
I'll be buried in my grave
and go home to my Lord and be free
They sang *I'm going to sit at the welcome table*
I'm going to live in the Governor's mansion
one of these days
I heard three mothers speak
who had made the President listen
and "almost cry, or he made like he was about to cry"
when they told him
how their homes had been dynamited

"It's not hard to be brave"
one of these mothers said
"but it's awful hard to be scared"
I expect to see her statue on a column in the square
in place of the Confederate soldier's
one of these days

Remember
slavery looked pretty permanent in 1858
when it had just five years to go
and now in 1964
the White Citizens' Councils and the Ku Klux Klan
think they can keep their kind of half-slave South forever
Their South isn't on the way out
It's already dead and gone
only they don't know it
They buried it themselves
in that earthwork dam near Philadelphia Mississippi
when they thought they were getting rid of the bodies

III

BESTRIDE
THE
NARROW
WORLD

BESTRIDE THE NARROW WORLD

"Why, man, he doth bestride the narrow world
Like a Colossus, and we petty men
Walk under his huge legs and peep about
To find ourselves dishonourable graves."
                    JULIUS CAESAR, *I, ii.*

We dangled them upon the edge a week
letting them savor death and then reprieved
them from their jeopardy a space. The style
is new. The abominations of his war
moved Lincoln to unmanly tears. Perhaps
he pondered Scripture overmuch. We too
bring God into our speeches. Fustian
we spout as well to cloak our naked sword
in words of righteous tone. Small matter if
the skeptical are unconvinced. We have
the countervailing force to make them cringe.
No power makes us stoop to parley. Proud
as pterodactyls in their prime are we,
mighty as mammoths whose unrivaled thews
the tundra binds in ice perpetual.

MARE NOSTRUM

Sea of ancient glory and modern misery
your waters are as stainless blue
as when your shores were unpolluted
by mankind
Liquid priestess of all times!
Vase of holy tears!
We call you ours
but rather we are yours

and when at last from Hellespont and Pharos
to where old Atlas groans beneath the world
only a vast necropolis confronts you
gazing vacant out to sea
you will mourn us with your surges
as a mother still rocks an infant
long after it has ceased to breathe

WISDOM OF THE ABBOT MACARIUS I

Said he: "I can no longer sanction
    any war for any purpose
        under God's sun or stars"
And they put him in chains

Said he: "I can no longer sanction
    any war for any purpose
        under God's sun or stars"
And they showed him the scaffold

Said he: "I can no longer sanction
    any war for any purpose
        under God's sun or stars"
And they laid his head on the block

Said he: "I can no longer sanction
    any war for any purpose
        under God's sun or stars"
And the ax fell

Whereupon the multitude fell silent
    thinking
        well
He could be right

BROTHER INNOCENT

Within your cloister
Brother Innocent
you beat your breast I know
for pagan days of yours when flesh was hot
and spilled itself in poems
concupiscent and unashamed
in front of all the world

Now
you make amends with nights upon your knees
where one small flame in all the darkness
burns before the sacred host
and days you spend in lowly ways
abased within your category
answering the bells
of monks whose sum of talent
comes to scarce a tithe of yours

Thought and act were one with you
even in days gone by
before the vision broke upon you
Murder was murder
your conscience said
in war as well as peace
and no fine words of prelate or of President
could make you see it otherwise
You bore no hand in slaughter
but chose instead a labor camp

Worse jails there could have been
but still
you were not free to leave
and when you were at last
five years had fled away
and women being what they are
flesh frail as yours or mine
you found your wife had been
well solaced in your absence

As pagans are wont to do
you left her
and took unto yourself another
who in her turn had been deceived
as you were cuckolded
Together you sought to wipe away
the tears of things
from one another's eyes
as if two people ever could

More sad your partner grew
and seeking out a healer of the mind
learned that her sickness lodged in guilt
for childhood faith forsaken
He counseled her to pluck
this buried faith up by the roots
like some choking weed
and burn it in the fire of reason
Instead she nourished it to bloom once more
and speedily grew well

And so a second time
you lost a wife
or did you only seem to lose her?
You found like refuge in the eternal rock
and ever deeper delve inside
as one who fleeing Caesar
threads labyrinths of catacombs
with holy taper guiding him
while in his ears
the Colosseum's muffled roars resound

A VETERAN'S DAY OF RECOLLECTION

We'd liberated Naples and the Wops
had come aboard to work cargo. This starving
Spik slipped a can of rations underneath
his lousy rags. We drilled him. At Marseilles
we mowed a stevedore down for pilfering
some Spam. The Battle of the Bulge was on,
V-bombs had knocked out Antwerp but the God
damned Frogs struck every ship of ours in port.
P-40's shot up Palermo for the hell
of it. Pinpoint objectives? Tenements!
Krauts wrecked Le Havre's docks and blew. The town
was open. Flying Fortresses blasted
it flat and left some thirty-thousand dead
allies of ours. Christ, how those ruins stank!
GI's in Germany went "one to shoot
and three to loot." We always gave
a Hershey to the frauleins that we ganged.

CONFORMITY MEANS DEATH
For Bertrand Russell

Our time's true saint he is, whose fealty
transcends the bounds of nation, tribe and clan,
embracing all who inhabit earth and their
inheritors. The voice we hear is more
than his. Through him the unborn of our loins
plead that we interpose our bodies now
between them and the Juggernaut we've built.
"Conformity means death!" No rhetoric
but starkest truth he speaks. Throw road blocks up
to Armageddon with your flesh. Besiege
the supine parliaments which veto peace
and cast their purchased votes for war. Let them
not sleep for your outcry. Fast unto death
if need be. Nail your picket signs upon
the doors of churches that usurp the cross
and grossly mock the One they feign to serve.
(He is not mocked but bides His awful time.)
Then rise! "Protest alone gives hope of life!"

AND EVER THE PYRES OF THE DEAD BURN THICK

Great Phoebus Apollo
unbend your silver bow
for mankind is weary of the slaughter
The proud the meek the foolish and the wise
the guilty and the innocent alike
die beneath your vengeful shafts
and never is there an end
to the hot blood smell

This woman now of Port Said
barefooted in her dress of rusty black
mounting a basket on her head
with cans of food raided from some sacked store
or flaming army dump
buys perhaps another week of life
for herself and orphaned brood
What is the crime of such as she
condemned to suffer so?

FOUR HAIKU FOR PETER

1. *El Camposanto*
Rich graves crowd near the shrine,
dressed green. Poor lie far off
in Franciscan brown.

2. *Slum Gothic*
Great empty nave.
Worship rocks store-fronts.
Peter's barque stranded on a reef.

3. *After Holy Communion*
Ite, missa est. Wealth
of cleanliness pours out.
Streets awash with filth.

4. *Picketing Hell Gate*
"Thou Shalt Not Kill!" Stand,
girl at the missile plant. Let men mock.
Stay His hand.

63

THE SHORE OF PEACE

War called you from the mill
whence come those powerful hands and frame
that make men fear you when you wish
the measured gait as if you balanced
heavy beams upon your shoulders
and roughened face
like iron cast in sand

You drove a tank
in all that clanking troop
that rolled a storm of dust
across Tunisia's desert hills
toward the shore where Carthage stood
before the Romans rooted out
that rival city
and salted down the ground
lest dragon's teeth once more
should spring up there

A score of centuries
and who could count the wars
since chariot wheels of Scipio Africanus
dug ruts where now your whirling tracks
churned through the alkali
but when you reached the narrow pass
foes broke from ambush and with fire
of mobile guns blasted your column
The medics found you crushed
and burned beside your gutted tank

But not so crushed nor yet so burned
that you were privileged to die
Your native strength and all the arts
whereby we drag men back from death
so they may live to kill again
these saved you and restored you

That shore you then assaulted
where once the youth of Athens came
wading from their galleys through the surf
They were the lucky ones who died
beneath the Syracusan swords
The rest wore chains and quarried stone
until the alien sun
bleached out their graveless bones

Life-jacketed you stood on deck
in the lee of that hostile coast
when sudden wings screamed down
and LST joined Greek trireme
below
Among the bodies washed ashore
was yours
but once again
your pulse kept shuddering on

And once again
the surgeons sutured and trepanned
with rubber-fingered skill
until they could pronounce you fit
for bloody work
and such you did along a road to Rome
that barefoot pilgrims used to walk

65

You helped obliterate
that hallowed abbey on its crag
the motherhouse of all the west
where Benedict himself had walked
in meditation on his Holy Rule
but our guns in blasphemous choir
chanted the hour of compline there
and Consummatum est was heard once more
beneath a blackened sky

From Germany laid waste
victorious you sailed for home
Home was the same but you were not
The vacant talk of friends
the well-filled envelope of weekly cash
the soothing flesh of women
none of these assuaged
the deep hurt in you
that for all their scopes and rays
the doctors could not diagnose

You found asylum then
where Wasatch peaks at evening
throw shadows on the fields of hay
You moved among the silent brothers
robed and cowled in coarsest brown
about your tasks in scullery and barn
as Benedict had bidden

Straw upon a board your bed
your fare but bread and barley water
with green stuff from the garden
Long before the dawn you rose

and after lauds and matins sung
fasting still you labored
while stars yet shone
with all the lustre of the Utah night

A year this was your world entire
a universe removed from men
and men's concerns for self
In all that while you spoke no word
save to confess your faults
Milking cows or dunging fields
your every act was prayer as deep
as psalms the choir monks chanted
within their carven stalls

What made you lay aside
your hooded Trappist habit?
What fiery-sworded angel
or was it conscience that forbade
you any longer to inhabit
this austere paradise?

You chose to make your home
with those who have no homes
the castaways of modern life
who in the roaring city are more lone
than hermits in their fastnesses
Immured are these each in his private hell
as on the flames they pour
the fuel alcohol and burn
themselves to deathlike sleep and wake
to pour and burn and die afresh

These sodden men
these women all degraded
you feed
as they file by with hanging heads
Each day you make the rounds
and beg on their behalf
stale loaves
fishes that stink
whatever men can't sell

From that same dish
whereon the wretched feed
you dine
That flophouse where they lay
their drunken heads each night
is also your hotel
Within your lumpy bed
you even share their bugs

And when one stifling afternoon
outside the Silver Dollar Bar
Willie the Weeper flips his lid
and shouts upon his knees
for God to strike him dead
while all his reeling cohorts circle
jeering round him on the sidewalk
you are the one who shoulders through the ring
to lift poor Willie up
and bear him tenderly away

68

UNDESIRABLES

"I lift my lamp beside the golden door."
Emma Lazarus. *Inscription for the Statue of Liberty.*

The lifted lamp is guttering, near spent
its fuel. Double-barred the golden door
which, when it opens, opens on a chain.
Where throngs poured through, police interrogate
each refugee, admitting but the few
who pass security and kiss the Book.
Carl Schurz would be excluded with his staunch
compatriots of Eighteen Forty-Eight
whose rebel blood caused liberty to grow
in their adopted land. Could Juárez get
a visa from the State Department? Would
the FBI clear Dvorak, known to be
in sympathies an anti-monarchist?
(Deport the New World Symphony!) Martí,
the Cuban foe of imperialism? Lorca,
the anti-fascist poet? These men were all
subversive as in earlier times Tom Paine,
Pulaski, Lafayette. The authorities
would surely bar such undesirables.

SOMEBODY WINS

Rain pelts the plastic-sheeted heap beside
the highway. One blue tennis shoe protrudes,
child-size. No child's the curving hip of her
mangled beneath, her car a jagged wreck.
The flinders of a second strew the swamp,
where moss-hung cypresses droop dankly down.

Attendants lead its blinded driver toward
the ambulance. Blood oozes from his lids.
Two cameras always at the ready, my
free-lancing friend leaps out and films the heap,
blue tennis shoe, the oozing lids, the feet
of spectators slogging around the corpse.
He climbs back in and we roar off again.
"That was a lucky break!" my friend exults.

SILENT IN DARIEN

He glimpses through dividing wire gold thighs
and shameless buttocks of *señoras gringas*
at play like children on the grass, his hell
their paradise. Bloat-bellied, puny sex
exposed, his brood clamors about the shack
tin-cans and cartons built. Girls who survive
turn assets, spreading rachitic legs to ease
off-duty Yanqui personnel. His sons
besides the pimping trade will follow such
pursuits as untaught hands may ply for rice
and beans, fare foreordained, lucky those days
they feed. In crystal shrines across the fence
one sees prime cuts of beef — *por Dios!* — milk,
the precious nuggets of the hen enclosed
in cunning boxes, bins of liquors, sweets,
rare nutriments whose flavors, even names
are mysteries, done up in shimmering foil.
The sky goes black as when a hurricane
lowers from the Caribbean. Unobscured
the sun glows bloody red. There will be wind.

JOSIAH TURNBULL TOOK NO PART IN POLITICS

Josiah Turnbull took no part in politics
toasting by the stove there
in his snug Philadelphia parlor
while the blizzard swirled
against the frosted panes
yes he congratulated himself
that he hadn't got mixed up
in anything political
but just attended to his own business

I wish I had lived in ancient Rome
in the days of the Gracchi
Josiah thought closing his Plutarch
ah with what dignity
the noble Romans went to their deaths
for their political beliefs
for liberty and justice
verily
Josiah thought knocking the ashes from his pipe
we have fallen upon evil days
and it behooves a man
to hold aloof
from the brawl in the marketplace
as I have done . . .

The door opened from the street
and a blast of cold
swept in from the hall
bending the lamp flames
Josiah could hear the redcoat Major
stamping the snow from his boots very carefully
before going upstairs to his room

the Major was always so correct
it was no hardship at all
to have him billeted there
and he paid for his lodging in gold

not like these Continentals
mechanics and country louts in stinking rags
with no gold or even silver to their names
but only paper
dirty worthless paper money
"not worth a Continental"
yes whatever the rights and wrongs of it might be
and there was much to be said on both sides
the British were the ones to do business with
and that very day
Josiah had made a most profitable bargain
with the British quartermaster
to deliver meat and grain for the garrison

there was the risk always
that the starving Continentals
encamped at the Valley Forge
might make a foray from their lair
and seize the farmers' wagons on the road
but it was Josiah's policy
to pay the farmers
only upon delivery of their produce in the city
so he did not stand to lose
whatever befell . . .

Josiah Turnbull stretched and yawned deeply
in his snug Philadelphia parlor
comfortably reflecting
that he took no part in politics

THE POLISHED CROSS

Inside the flawless chapel
for which the architect received a prize
Christ in low relief on granite
falls under a polished cross

Above the portal Mary mothers
a childish cluster while across
the terraced lawn within the offices
all gleaming glass the staff is gathered

"Embarassing our topic for today
but we must squarely face it
The sin of sodomy is rife among
our boys and drastic measures are required

Above all vigilance ... a constant watch
Make sure by peering underneath the door
two boys are never found to occupy
one toilet ... Keep an eye upon the showers

Patrol the ballfield lest they hide
behind the backstop ... Sneak beside the gym
and come upon them by the fire door
where weeds grow high and thick

Don't let a single pair of boys
get out of sight an instant
The kind we have here are abnormal
incorrigibly vicious

73

Let no new counselor imagine
he can accomplish anything
with kindness for the boys will think
it is the mark of weakness

Such men quit soon we find
or else we have to let them go
These boys are future criminals
and all they understand is force

Before we leave the subject
you might take down these names
of boys we have some reason to believe
corrupt the others ... first Gonzales ...

You'll find these Mexicans are all
inclined that way ... Don't trust them ...
Jackson next ... Most Negroes are alike ...
Sex mad and if they can't get girls

They'll take what they can get ...
Antonelli ... Italians are hot-blooded ...
Smathers O'Rourke and Jankovich ...
Degenerate stock in these three cases ..."

Within the flawless chapel
for which the architect received a prize
a rough-hewn granite Christ
is nailed upon a polished cross

74

THE SEARCH FOR TRUTH

Do I have freedom here
to search for truth and teach it to my students
the way I used to
before the oath and all these things came in?
Freedom is such a nebulous word
I don't know what you mean exactly
You'd have to define your terms
I teach the way I always have
but you know how it is
one goes on learning
one grows more experienced
one's taste becomes more disciplined
one realizes that the young
are prone to take things literally
and so a gradual approach to truth
is sometimes indicated
It seems to me a choice of values
is involved in this whole question
of so-called academic freedom
The public hires us to teach the young
Well and good
Would it then be fair for us
to betray the public trust
and teach our students what the public
does not approve of?
Clearly not and furthermore
we are dependent on the public
for our support
At last our salaries begin to match
those of professionals in other fields
and should we jeopardize these gains
with ill-conceived quixotic claims

to be a law unto ourselves?
Each year the legislature votes for us
another three per cent increase in pay
and look around you at these buildings
our new gymnasium our stadium
These mean we have the public's confidence
I wouldn't want to see this sacrificed
I don't think you would either
My attitude about the Mitchell case?
My opinion is that Dr. Mitchell
for all his undoubted brilliance
is not a man of tact and showed less judgment
than a full professor should possess
The police force as we know is far from honest
riddled with corruption if you please
What city's force is any better?
But to send one's students over town
sticking their noses into everything
with questionnaires
not even leaving out the brothels!
This was too much
He put the institution and his colleagues
to use a vulgar term upon the spot
with that investigation of the links
between police and prostitutes
That kind of thing is not our business
We should concern ourselves
with the eternal verities
and not the ephemeral passing show
We see events in true perspective only
generations after they occur
and all this hue and cry
over academic freedom
will surely seem a tempest in a teapot

a century or two from now
Of course it is a shame that Dr. Mitchell
had to go
He'd published many books
and was a credit to the faculty
May you quote me?
Oh no indeed!
I meant no criticism by my remark
It was a wise decision to dismiss him
I just meant . . .
Really I didn't mean a thing
but Mitchell was my friend
Don't quote me though
I want that off the record

FINISHING SCHOOL

A ten-foot fence that's topped with barbed wire strands
surrounds this finishing school. In star-marked cars
the girls are fetched by uniformed escorts.
Sad debutantes! Lovers you shall not lack.
Trapped female animals surpass the male
in viciousness. To frustrate vigilance
and woo each newcomer with arts practiced
on Sappho's isle is all their frenzy here.
The pool's a passion tank. About each pair
of furtive amorists fair mermaids sport
to screen their throes of love. Fine scenery
encompasses the school and visitors
exclaim. The picture windows when kicked out
by inmate heels make serviceable dirks,
stilettos, spears, from which psychologists
shrink back, and even deputies with guns.

YOURS IN THE BONDS

Brother, your appeal's at hand. Our house
through long neglect decays. We must infuse
at once and massively the cash to heal
time's ravages, perpetuate the breed
we're noted for, oarsmen and athletes of
the bottle, clean-cut types whose fathers sit
on the Exchange. If we decline to act
the university will seize our house,
restore and lease it back to us at cost
of cherished principle. We might be forced
to take a Jew, Negro, or Indian.
Must we then foot the bill? A bitter choice!
Fat though our winnings from portfolios
and corporations we manipulate,
it's most repugnant to our principles
to make donations not deductible.
We joined our dearly beloved fraternity
to turn a profit, not incur a loss.
It was our lofty object to latch on
to lads who counted in the world, scions
of Munsingwear or Listerine or U.
S. Steel. The secret grip, the ritual
and all that garbage went along, quaint old
survivals from an age of squares who took
this jovial fraternal bit for real.
In 1853 Grandfather joined
at Williams, then a hick establishment.
The bumpkin "Prex" sat on a log and you
upon the other end and that, they claimed,
was education. Lots of good it did
Grandfather, all his wasted life a parson
who shared his pittance with the poor. When Father

matriculated at Cornell, Ezra's
egalitarian injunctions still
prevailed. A loutish school. The chapter house
was just a clapboard shack on Lake Street hill.
Later a turreted mansion was acquired
to accommodate a band increasingly
elite. In martial Teddy's times it burned
and boys were trapped. The brothers braved the flames
in vain attempts at rescue. They too died.
A note on White House stationery bears
high witness to their heroism. I
would not detract nor could I add a word.
Suffice it that the house burned down with loss
of life deplored by all. Insurance was
in force, the Lord be praised. Alumni dug
another bundle up and reared the pile
where I, a double legacy, was pledged,
initiated, taught to swill and wench.
Here I absorbed contempt for scholarship,
bitch goddess worship and a fake mythos
that made me dream myself superior
to all beyond the pale of our sweeping
greensward. Tricked out in coonskin coats and suits
from Brooks, we saw the world as our private
demesne to plunder rightfully while our
inferiors stood helplessly aside.
You ask me, brother, for my honest views.
My voice is for abandoning this relic
or willing it to the authorities to do
with as they wish. The brotherhood we preached
and practised was a fraud. Not love but hate
united us -- the vilest kind that hates
a man because his name or skin is wrong,
oblivious to what at heart he is.

ON ACQUIRING A CISTERCIAN BREVIARY
(For Father M. Louis, O.C.S.O.)

Long cloistered these old volumes that my hands
profane. Rubbed spines spell golden seasons. *Pax
intrantibus!* How many hidden men
dipped honeycomb from hence and Samson-thewed
robustly strove till sepulture beside
the abbey church! Each has his sombre cross
of naked iron with laconic plaque,
sacerdos and *conversus* leveled quite,
Dom James whose tassel was abbatical
and bearded Frater Hyacinth who baked.
And will they rise triumphantly in choir
all faults expunged? These rubricated leaves
were thumbed by novices who now lie here.
But flowery tropes the prophecy and pledge,
a travesty on truth which holds no hope
for them? If so, how came they to be strong,
these silent monks? May desert rocks fill men
with food or venom work their cure? Embrace
such paradox who can. These books I'll have.

TURN OF THE YEAR

Sea-serpents churn the sky and octopi
twine slimy tentacles about the firs.
Aleutian-bred, the equinoctial storm
abolishes that composition all
cerulean and gold which summer brushed
upon the coastal ranges. Raging gusts

squander the coinage of my Royal Annes,
minted but yesterday. A glint of sun
flees down the slopes and vanishes like fawns
startled among the apples — a dappled flash
and over the fence into the redwood grove.
Siva, destruction's king, was multi-limbed
as these sequoias, choreographers
of death, aghast against the stricken sky.
        Morning Star Ranch, Sebastopol California, 1956.

COMMERCIAL VEHICLES PROHIBITED

An Eden for the citizens who'd jeered
his dream McLaren conjured up from dunes.
We thread his pungent eucalyptic aisles
by tandem bicycle. Sun laced with fog
intoxicates, elixir of the air.
The castaways from Czernowicz and Czestochowa
stand watch around the sailing basin but
never a barque hauls round to their rescue.
"Welcome Dentists' Convention" succulents
declare. Fat dahlias droop. Lank bison too.
A languorous November, gold as May,
has tricked a rhododendron into bloom.
A shamefaced chauffeur walks a coiffeured poodle.
The pseudo-Grecian peristyle attracts
its quota of photographic devotees.
A maple with each scarlet leaf intact
flames on the waters where one idling swan
redeems a flock of ducks hustling for crusts.
        San Francisco, 1957.

THE MASTER OF YELLOW PLUM MOUNTAIN

The Master on the night wind scented death,
his own that sought him out. Within his cell
he sat serene awaiting the encounter
when hubbub arose from the scriptorium
shattering his contemplation of last things.
Contentious monks were sharpening a point
of doctrine. Such overweening disciples shamed
the master, he reflected, fanging the Way
of Truth with tigerish disputes. He could
foresee the tonsured brawlers around his bier
all snatching for his robe, the sacred garment
that Bodhi-Dharma wore from India
when he brought first the Buddha's luminous words
across Himalayas to the Middle Realm.
Foreknowledge made the Master flinch. He should
now pass the robe to whom he chose, as once
he had been vested by his predecessor
of blessed memory. But which of these
proud meretricious monks would not debase it?
In his extremity he thought of one
new to the brotherhood, scion of men
who, yoked with crusted buckets, at back doors
begged excrement of close-stools which they hawked
to peasants for enriching garden plots.
For all his forebears' noisome trade, the gate
was opened to this man, the monastery
being short of kitchen hands. The most abject
of scullions now he pounded husks from rice
to fatten nobler bellies than his own.
The Master rang and had him fetched. "Leave us!"

ORDER FORM

To: RED MOUNTAIN EDITIONS,
     BOX 7331-A, MOUNTAIN BROOK STATION,
     BIRMINGHAM, ALABAMA 35223.

POETRY BY JOHN BEECHER

▶▶▶▶▶▶▶▶▶◀◀◀◀◀◀◀◀◀

PLEASE SEND ME (Check below.)

❊❊❊ TO LIVE AND DIE IN DIXIE ❊❊❊
☐ Clothbound $5. ☐ Paper $2.

❊ REPORT TO THE STOCKHOLDERS ❊
☐ Clothbound $3.

OTHER PUBLICATIONS: (List.)

Alabama Residents Add
5½% Sales Tax

❖❖❖❖❖❖❖❖❖❖❖❖❖❖❖❖❖❖❖❖❖❖❖❖❖

I enclose ☐ check ☐ money order in the amount of $ . . . .

Name . . . .

Address . . . .

City . . . .

State, Zip Code . . . .

OTHER POETRY BY JOHN BEECHER

PHANTOM CITY

The Old West: what's left. Portraiture at once mordant &
compassionate of a town & its people. Beautifully printed
in imported hand-set types; original blocks. One hundred
copies numbered & signed by the poet, cloth, $5. Regular
edition: clothbound $3; soft hand-sewn wrappers $2.

HERE I STAND
Twice A Year Press, New York, 1941
"It has the stuff of social reality in it . . . it leaves a scar
on our consciousness." Max Lerner.
Numbered & signed edition $5.00.   Clothbound. $2.75.

AND I WILL BE HEARD
Twice A Year Press, New York, 1940
The poet's first publication, "Really a document . . . always
interesting, always provocative." Louis Untermeyer.
                                        Paper. $1.00.

ALL OF THE ABOVE-LISTED BOOKS MAY BE
ORDERED FROM RED MOUNTAIN EDITIONS,
BOX 7331-A, MOUNTAIN BROOK STATION,
BIRMINGHAM, ALABAMA 352

The startled messenger withdrew at this
command. The dying Master slowly rose,
removing from his back the Dharma robe
and spread it over deep-bowed, trembling shoulders.
"Go, lest your holy brethren and their knives
discover your investiture. Avoid
the roads and seek the mountain fastnesses.
Your heart will know the day you must return
to men and teach." That night the Master died.
Missing the robe, the enraged community
in arms sought to apprehend the fugitive
but he had vanished in the highest snows.

THE SIXTH GREAT PATRIARCH DECLINES

His crabbed brush indites: "Dread Lord! Your scroll's
superb calligraphy dazzles my eyes,
the eloquence of your minister my ears.
With tongue more silken than his gown
he bids me quit these rocky slopes for your
imperial palace. Could such inducements sway
my mind you'd gain another clown at court.
Your majesty mistakes his man. My bag
contains no magic tricks, no paper snakes
to affright the people or to make them clap.
The sutras are my only store, from them
I draw my poor powers, this robe the badge
of my superior emptiness. Husker
of rice was I. The Master for a sign
clothed me, the least of men, with Dharma. You,
I hear, are prone to heap old ivories,
patinaed bronze, pomegranite girls, eunuchs,
gold trinkets, jade, translucent porcelain.

Would you augment your hoard with my person,
another on the random list of self-
indulgences, a man clothed in the robe
once worn by Bodhi-Dharma, sealed thereby
both saint and sage, the wonder of the time?
Must I for strings of cash augur tea-cups,
discourse of voices heard upon the mountains,
pose mystical conundrums for myself
to crack like lichee nuts? Most august sire!
I must decline to be your holy fool.
Foolish I am in truth but keep my house
amongst my thousand monks where it is hid.
Besides the Dharma on my back wears thin
and ragged. In pity of my nakedness
the beggars at your gate might toss me coins."

THE CAMALDOLESE COME TO BIG SUR

White-habited hermits pace fog that streams
landward at compline bell. The ambrosial coast
harbors flesh-eaters, a poet's evil dreams.
Their ordure smears the cliffs. Now Jeffers lies
earthfast save prayer of these ransom his ghost,
so avid of dark. Cowled fathers, exorcise
his doomed lovers. Asperse, blest hands, these great
headlands commanding sapphire plenitudes.
Where blood-stained phantoms neigh and ululate,
let seraphim deploy hushed multitudes.

DRAGONFLY

His wings refract the sun; their arabesques
are intricate as damascene; he rides
the tremors of the heat above the creek.
The dragonfly's all azure. With his mate
he couples in the air and sails elate
and unabashed before his smiling Lord.

PUNTA DE LOS LOBOS MARINOS

He'd crawled up in the cove to die alone.
When we came near he raised his head, his eyes
blank disks. Flies fed on pus that dripped from them.
Flies swarmed upon his flippers. Feverish,
he shook. "There's nothing we can do but let
old nature take her course," the ranger said
and sauntered off. The young sea lion dropped
his heavy head and coughed sepulchrally.
"Pneumonia," I ventured. "He needs a shot."
"I'd give him one," a man remarked, "except
he'd sink his teeth in me." "You're an M.D.?"
"That's right," he said. "I'll hold him for you then."
I gripped that bullet head with both my hands.
Hide bent the needle double but the dose
went in, good for a week. The creature roared
as youngsters do when stuck. The doctor wiped
his ruined needle. "Can't do harm," he said,
"and maybe he'll get well." Next day the beach
was bare. The pack was sunning on the rocks
offshore. Some slithered in the Caldron's rips,
outwitting clashing seas and granite teeth.
We guessed one lucky youngster was home free.

ZION CANYON: EVENING

Named for a man, the Virgin river wears
an accidental grace. Her trout-rife reaches
darkle in the shadowed lees of colossi
whose thews of rosy stone she carved in moods
subliminal during her Maenad past.
What Byzantine basilica for all
its glittering glooms and fluted chrysoprase
but shrinks to bauble-scale measured by this
obdurate ecstasy of soaring rock?
Dour Mormon farm folk, first of our breed, fell
down on their knees before these high altars
that take the sunset molten on their planes.
The canyon fills with darkness but the light
lingers over Zion like an aureole.

BODEGA HEAD
For Barbara

On these miles of sand the cold sea beats
watched only by me as I walk
Wheeling around me the gulls
lustfully shriek over corpses of fish
washed up by the poisonous waters
Ship's timbers all shivered and wan
lie about on the beach and stir into mind
the death of a schooner on the offshore reef
Borne here across infinite ocean
the jade-green float of a Japanese fishnet
gleams in a tangle of seaweed

86

The tide withdraws and on the dampened sand
I see dim tracks of a girl's bare feet
curving and weaving awhile with the wave-line
then vanishing over the dunes
Dare I follow and come on her there
in some deep cleft of the dunes
nested down warm out of the sea wind
and the fog's raw breath?

A DEATH AT SEA

Off Jupiter light we rolled our beams
till Gulfstream indigo supplanted green swells.
Line paid out, the club-thick rod fast-socketed,
the wicked lure thrashed up
a witching rainbow in our wake.
The sailfish when she struck careened me to the rail,
line screaming the reel. Enginewards the skipper
leaped churning his craft astern.
Reeling in, I felt the sailfish rage for liberty
as if electric shock ran through my bones,
and when she jumped
her parabolic fin flashed nacreous in the sun.
We fought an hour upon that indigo sea
until I staggered on the deck
gulping for breath and she
lay lashing wearied by the stern.
The gaff bit deep into her iridescent side
and she shone an instant like a captured mermaid in the air
but in a frenzied spasm
tore her flesh free from hooks and gaff
and dove to die in her own element.

OUR THOUGHTS ARE FREE

Listen!
Ralph is going to sing for us
Die Gedanken sind frei
Oh that's the one I love so much
It means *Our thoughts are free*
Such a message for today!
Look there at those Williamses!
What gall of them to come!
They claim they can't afford a contribution
to our club this year
and yet they have the nerve
to show their faces at our picnic!
Did you hear what Bunny Williams said
to Miriam?
She told Miriam she thought our country
was not the only one to blame for wars
around the world the atom race and all
She said the Soviet Union was almost
as bad as we are
Yes she did!
That's exactly what she said
Her husband Henry's just as anti-everything
as Bunny is
The government purged him from his job
because he'd fought in Spain
the International Brigade you know
and now he's selling hearing aids
but Paul believes that's just a blind
Paul put out the word to keep away
from Henry Williams
Paul heard him criticize the Party once
and hasn't trusted him for years

Paul says those hearing aids
that Henry carries in that bag of his
to make you think he sells them
probably are hidden dictaphones
that take down every word you say
Don't even speak to him
the dirty stool-pigeon!
Oh Ralph that song was so inspiring!
Encore! Encore!

SELF PORTRAIT IN A BAD LIGHT

My stripling authors flee the room to rub
congenial elbows in those dives where false
identities will pass. Cassocks withdraw
to contemplation of reforms. (But not
too radical nor yet too near the quick
of clerical privilege!) Dare I adjure
my Muse to plain of social wrongs in such
precarious circumstance? Must I be schooled,
veil plain speech in symbolic fog, costume
polemics for a merry morris dance,
practice new types of ambiguity,
and baffle those who sniff out heresy?
These shifts are common to the trade and steer
the prudent to snug haven when the gale's
a-starboard, blustery. No matter. The old
dog's teeth, to vary tropes, grow blunt. His eye
is blear. He shows more energy in dreams,
waggling his paws, than questing on all fours.
Who would heed his bark, grown querulous and faint?

IF I FORGET THEE, O BIRMINGHAM!

I.
Like Florence from your mountain.
Both cast your poets out
for speaking plain.

II.
You bowl your bombs down aisles
where black folk kneel
to pray for your blacker souls.

III.
Dog-torn children bled
A, B, O, AB as you.
Christ's blood not more red.

IV.
Burning my house to keep
them out, you sowed wind. Hear it blow!
Soon you reap.

90

A HUMBLE PETITION TO THE PRESIDENT OF HARVARD

I am, sir, so to speak, "a Harvard man."
In legendary times I lugged my green
baize bag across the Yard to sit while fierce
Professor Kittredge paced his podium
in forkéd snowy beard and pearl-grey spats,
mingling his explications with his views
obscurantist on life and letters. Texts
prescribed for us were caponized. Prince Hamlet
made no unseemly quips anent the thighs
Ophelia spread for him nor did that poor
crazed beauty sing the naughty songs for which
she's celebrated. Nice young men were we
in Kitty's class. Extra-curricular
our smut -- Old Howard queens of bump and grind,
the Wellesley girls who warmed our chambers. Such
the Harvard I recall: Widener's great hive,
whose honeyed lore we rifled and bore off
on index cards, all nutriment destroyed;
the home of Henry Wadsworth Longfellow;
dank mournful halls; an ill-proportioned pile
commemorating boys who'd marched away
to die for causes the professors had
endorsed, knowing infallibly which side
God and their butter were upon. Our boot-
legger was Polish. Christened Casimir
Zwijacz he'd changed his name to Lawrence Lowell
after fair Harvard's president. Ambushed
and shot by high-jackers who coveted
his rot-gut load, Lowell barrelled his truck
back from Cape Cod and, bandaged bloodily,

made punctual deliveries to all
his Cambridge clientele, fresh lustre shed
upon an honored name. *Per aspera!*
Nostalgic reminiscences brought on
by your most recent bulletin. I learn
of your "Commitment to the Modern", penned
expressly for Old Grads by Lionel
Trilling, D. Litt., a masterpiece, I thought,
of academic prose, so clear and yet
so dark. It cheers me that you do not change
at Harvard, like *castrati* whose voices
retain their boyish purity. Trilling
delights me with his cadenced double-talk.
"The radical," says he, and dares to add
"subversive" in a breathless tone, is like
to be predominant among the forces of
our time. Already on the student mind
(so impatient of the rational) this force
works powerfully. Oppose it, counsels he,
in order that it may grow strong and strike
deep roots. "Bland tolerance," he trills, "subverts"
subversion, makes it wither on the vine.
The way to nurse dissent is to impose
conformity -- the logic's Lionel's --
and carefully exclude dissenters from
the faculty. Would we aid William Blake
to mew his mighty youth? Deny stipends.
Give ninnies suck at Alma Mater's teats.
Wean Blake. Choose Doodle in his stead as Poet
in Residence lest William be suborned
by excess of ease and lick the arses that
require booting. The University
of Hard Knocks is the proper berth for such

obstreperous geniuses. "When we are scourged,
they kiss the rod, resigning to the Will
of God," as Swift observed of moralists
like Trilling. Fend from me, I beg you, sir,
offers of chairs magnates endow. Waylay
me with no teaching sinecure. (Degrees
sufficient to impress the Dean are mine.)
Summon me never to recite my verse
before a convocation in my honor
nor to appear in doctoral costume
as orator at Commencement. Such coddling,
as Trilling rightly says, would work my ruin.
Let me forever cope with penury
and cold neglect. Let me be ostracized
for practising ideals you fine folk
are given to prating of at ceremonies.
Do what you please with me defunct. Put up
a plaque. Dissect my corpse in seminars.
Transmogrify my bones to index cards.
Hang my dead portrait in the library
and crucify your living rebels still.

93

Also by John Beecher:

REPORT TO THE STOCKHOLDERS
& OTHER POEMS

MR Press photo-offset replica of original limited edition, award-winning book. Handsomely bound in full cloth: $3.00

". . . this volume . . . deserves a place upon the shelves of all libraries . . ." — LIBRARY JOURNAL.

"*Report to the Stockholders* is a very fine book of poetry, the old, outspoken, direct, hard hitting verse that people are apparently forgetting how to write. I find the poems tremendously moving, very convincing and persuasive." — Thomas Merton.

"Beecher . . . is a poet of integrity and power writing in the core tradition of creative America . . . he belongs in the same company as Thoreau, Emerson, Whitman, Melville and Robert Frost." — August Derleth.

"Of his doubly creative work as poet and printer, the capstone thus far is *Report to the Stockholders*." — FRONTIER.

"Read Beecher's six line epitaph on the black bodies found in the embers of a Negro church. You cannot be the same again." — THE CHRISTIAN CENTURY.

". . . this is not personal protest at all, but a holy rage at the enemy at home and a mine of tenderness for the insulted and injured, the jailed and blacklisted." — Thomas McGrath.

"Beecher . . . has searched for and discovered his own American speech, his own trenchant yet moving form, creating a pointed poetry that stands tiptoe in our times . . . The styles of Hikmet, Brecht, Neruda, Andrade, Aliger, Yevtushenko and Beecher vary greatly but each excites healthy response, each performs a particular function, each is needed. . . . Here is a writer with an invincible social instinct. Beecher will be even more important tomorrow because he is actively and responsibly attempting to shape a more progressive tomorrow. His poems constantly reflect his deep commitment . . . an almost lifelong engagement in art and in the streets of America." — Leslie Woolf Hedley.